BETTING ON THE NIGHT

BETTING ON THE NIGHT

poems by

Dennis Held

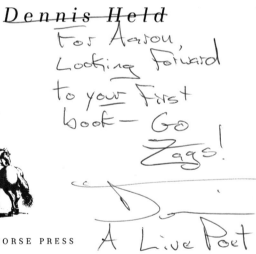

For Aaron,
Looking forward
to your first
book — Go
Zags!

A Live Poet

LOST HORSE PRESS

SANDPOINT • IDAHO

Library of Congress Cataloging-in-Publication Data

Held, Dennis.
Betting on the Night: poems/by Dennis Held.—1st ed.
Sandpoint, Idaho: Lost Horse Press, 2001.
p. cm.
ISBN 0-9668612-8-0 (alk. paperback)
I. Title.

PS3608.E43 B4 2001
811'.6—dc21

First Edition
Second Printing 2003

Cover Art by Dale Tucker
Book Design by Christine Holbert

This book is dedicated to
Claire Davis and *Brian Wroblewski*

Methinks we have hugely mistaken this matter of Life and
Death. Methinks that what they call my shadow here on earth
is my true substance.

—Ishmael, *Moby Dick,* or *The Whale*

'The ship! The hearse!—the second hearse!' cried Ahab from
the boat; 'its wood could only be American!'

—Captain Ahab, *Moby Dick,* or *The Whale*

CONTENTS

Betting on the Night

Season of Our Remains

Expense of the Heart

The Black Road

VAN GOGH IN MONTANA

I

He polkas a two-step flop out the boxcar door
of the four o'clock freight from Butte
and Bill, the yard bull, says watch your step
so he does, all the way into town, careful

to tramp down the puddle ice that barks
like a circus seal. Across one rail, eyes
wide open, an orange and black tabby
sliced in two, still surprised at the light.

But Vince knows he can't save anybody,
least of all himself. Hell's already too full
of heroes. There's one now: a doughboy
who's only lobbing a snowball, not

a grenade, stranded on a pedestal before
the county courthouse that rings four-thirty.
Smudges of woodsmoke usher in the dusk.
He pulls down his watchcap over an ear

and sets out west for color, where two yellow
hills succumb to the slow-moving ploy
of a deeper huckleberry light, where
outside of town a long field of solemn

grain stacks drift off, set loose
like cattle seen running in fever dreams.
If he's not careful, he'll be gone as soon
as the sun, and the moon's already up,

betting on the night.

II

Finally, for winter's sake, he had come
to trust the undiluted cold, to absorb the many
intricate and particular pains of gray ice,

but now this changling wind—"chinook"—
that strips the hides from snowbanks and sends
the pale light everywhere shimmering.

Tough-minded song sparrows gloat
in vaporous trills above stray hounds that run
the tracksides, growl and tussle over

bones and gristle of doe and fawn.
Vince shivers, works a trick of light to help
shuck off the regular tug toward the sure,

laborious weight of loss that courses
through the damp air that is just now dense
with the unqualified love of decay.

III

Someone will name a child for him today.

He scrabbles along a scalloped jawbone
of ice that juts deep into the clotted river.
He follows. Back toward town, the grain

elevator's gunmetal blue rhymes with the sky.
Even the church steeple is pointless, domed
as any bullet: Fog brings down the cross.
A packet of geese cobbles over, pushing a klaxon

lament as they head for the mountains that break
in whitecaps, churlish waves braiding away
to the scar of horizon, the only seam, only border
of this tossed-off land. The pigeons assemble

for stray chaff, and night sets up its final picnic:
tablecloth of stars, one bright tea cup.

DIASPORA

Day thirteen of painting
the House from Hell,
six bucks an hour and not
a flat patch of ground
for the ladders,
forty-foot peaks, adrenalin thumps
around every bend when I find
the nest the owner's been grousing about
a neat triangle
of bricks

knocked out
in a safe spot, shaded by the eaves
and a pair of rambunctious sparrows
the owner wants *out*: the racket
at four in the morning,
the rucus of all those young . . .

I crawl out the attic window, plant
a shaky foot on the sill and wedge
the other maculate workboot
in the steep pitch
of a dormer,
packing an arsenal
of tools: screwdriver,
needle-nose, a long dinner fork,
hauling out tufts of interwoven down
and Christmas tinsel, frayed
cigarette butts and bits
of baling twine.

The parent birds curse demurely
from the locust trees, mending from
branch to branch as I try to hook the nest,

probing gently
            with the fork
at first, then pliers, to still the shrill bells
in the throats of the fledglings
I hear now, deep in the wall.
I toss out a small twist of nest—

so light, so slow,

it drifts like a cradle
rocking.

And one by one I find them
well back in the dark, a thin hood of skin
still veiling their eyes, beaks agape

and no god
on the way.

Men behind beards and those thorny hedges,
  women shouldering a life's worth
of kids wherever they go, spilling out infants
   from milk-stained sweaters and winnowing
their way past tin homes that spill the all
   too-obvious busted-down washers and not
much going on and beer, and the railroad
  underpass with requisite indigents trailing
their cardboard aspirations past the boarded-up
  lumber mill—no more checks exchanged
for slower northside digits—past the collapsed
   automotive hopes cruising forever on cinder
blocks, birch stumps, a gaping Comet
   canted on a tricycle facing down the chainlink
playground fence, all of it indifferent beneath
  a skiff of early snow to the one who still
drifts the infield, filled with grace,
   holding forth in all those lost western dialects
of beauty and ruin, his stone in St. Mary's cemetery
  cradled between butressed maple roots
near a row of nuns with men's names, limestone
  crosses dissolving contritely in the rain,
the unnecessary black, cast-iron spikes of the fence . . .
   loathing and absence cost nothing to drive through
although the mud sticks to my tires and grafts
  to the feet of hungry kids already puckering
back in a clot, circled against anything
  from outside the northside, or in.

TURNING TO ROSES: MONTANA WAR
MEMORIAL, MISSOULA, 1990

A balding man, young but old enough to have Vietnam in him
　　　　rocks an open stroller before the monumental bronze
figures: an oversized GI, larger than life, his boots cast
　　　　a bit rough, staring up uncomprehending into the face
of a muscular angel, forearms straining to haul
　　　　them both aloft. He runs a hand down the soldier's cold
rifle, surveys the gardens, the well-trimmed lawns,
　　　　the one-hundred roses laid out in parallel plots:
Hotshot, Fireball, Holiday, Remembrance. He turns to
　　　　the names of roses, turns to the roses themselves.
From nowhere a sprinkler throws a rope of water
　　　　at the stroller and the startled child wails and wails.
The father lifts his daughter, holds her quiet for now
　　　　under the sheltering needles of the orderly pines.

AUBADE FOR A GARMENT BAG

Dawn's distant apparition:
                a breakdancing
                        body-sized bag,
the seventh veil alive,
              two twists and a shimmying
                  writhe alongside the bleak
                      and songless Montana
highway,
gravel-tossing pirouettes
              that pull him over
                  with a breazy backbeat,
              a breathless chant
of embodied rhythm
aeolian princess
rising in diesel
thermals delighted,
            transluscent peignoir swelled,
            plush champagne grape,
                soft belly Rubens-round,
            spilling upward again
            and again, filled
with dust or
indifference
or possibly
love
and when
it's finally too much,
            when he feels his distant hand
                clasping the door latch

a cabover Pete
rolls by with a
                         downshifted wink
                         of black smoke
          a swaggering two-trailer
                  wiggle
                              and you
are gone for good,
sucked into the impatient
vacuum of longing
                              and he
is alone,
grinning like a fool,
a broken-down fox
with a mouthful of green
grapes and a taste
for sour.

COLD MORNING: WEITAS CREEK, IDAHO

I

Steve reinvents the air
with form and intent
as he puffs up the hill
from the creek toting
two full water jugs,
smiling somehow wider
than his face when he sees
the haloed mug of coffee
lifted from the new-made
campfire. Someone says
"Blessings on the many
warming things" as rings
of mist lift from the firs
and the first thin light
slaps him full in the mouth,
candles his breath:
sunrise this day
is surely no accident.

II

Willows offer up
       dissolving gowns

                     of mist

       Johnagon Creek
             alert and clucking
       at the gravel:

Look alive look look alive
no alms have I but a camp coffepot
glazed black
and rude socks
to rinse in summer
snowmelt and scrub
with particoloured bits
of flint and red granite
then a match-head fleck
of soap worked down past the heel
and up through the toe, a blood spot

fading with the rub
then off to steep
in a clearwater rinse,
walk the kettle up the ridge
to baptise a ponderosa pine.
No wonder
the cutthroat rose
the next morning,
no wonder
that sun.

SEASON OF OUR REMAINS

He handed me matches from his cigarette pack,
                    hair slicked up
into that blond fifties wave, the accidental dad with six
                    boys and now two
girls, they could finally quit.
"Keep an eye out, it's windy, you hear?"
After supper dishes are done I can burn
garbage, November chill
                    pressed back,
                         the dark falling
                                away in jumps
                                and sparks, alone
                         in a bull's-eye of light with
                    a bread bag draped over
                    a stick just so, dripping liquid fire . .

But now to unearth
the bathroom bag
with a sodden bundle
wrapped in toilet paper,
a package I was sure
came from my mother,
blood perhaps shed
for me, for my father.
What other wounds
did she hide I wondered
as it all caught fire until
even the blood and stars

and moon were aflame
and the barrel slowly
filled with our ashes.

I

      At Lannon Quarry a mile from home,
Two uniformed men dump a drum
      Overboard and lower bullhead minnows
In wire-mesh cages—freshwater canaries,
      To die when the poison hits bottom.
Hundreds of problem bluegills—"stunted"—
      Twitch the surface. "We're going
To manage the lake for trout."
      Knowing better, the crows move in.

II

Sunday nights, Land-O-Lakes
      Double-A hardball in Lannon,
Abandoned limestone quarries
      Behind the outfield fence that sells
Schwister Ford and Mib's and Viv's Tap.
      Chasing down homers and long
Foul balls we duck the rusting
      Steamshovels and shin-slicing wire,
Sometimes diving on a dare despite true
      Stories of cousins who never came back.
Before the games, the janitor pulls
      A fogger billowing a scarf of pure
DDT into the evening air shocked blue
      By stadium lights. We spin through
The oily smoke playing Statue Maker
      While dads and grandpas
Nurse shorties of Pabst.

III

        A skull on the can, my dad
Sprays burdock and Russian thistle.

        I kneel close, wanting to touch the spikes
Already curling back toward some blackened past.

        The poison makes the plant kill itself
From inside. One Saturday my dad cleans

        The boss's indoor pool with acid and runs
Outside, heaving, face slack and yellow,

        Then back in with a plastic bag over his head
Ten breaths at a time, to finish the job.

IV

The asthma's helped by blue
        Pills that make me
Shake and a red
        Inhaler. "In goes
The good air, out
        Goes the bad"
We learned at school
        And I wonder what
Inside us turned
        Sweet air to poison.

LAST NAMES

–for Carl von Linné

> That which has been successfully defined
> has been successfully killed.
> —*Christmas Humphreys*

I

      Sorry, Linnaeus, even *your* name
Got the treatment, lowbrow sloppy
      Swedish sweetened into Latin—
Carolus, for Christ's sake—
      But maybe you deserve it,
The specific son of a bitch who drew
      Boxes around all the living.
Not 200 years ago you gave us
      The monikers for everything alive
(Species, genus and family)
      The first step in owning them all:
Ursus arctos horribilis, grizzly bear
      Faggot idiot snail darter bitch.
The rest is easy. We're naming ourselves.

II

In third grade, I fell in love
      With the confusing euglena:
Even science books didn't know
      Whether it was plant or animal,
"A green protozoan with a distinctive
      Red pigment spot" that explained

The dictionary story: *Glene,*
　　　　Latin for pupil of the eye,
Cousin by sound to Eugene,
　　　　Dad's youngest brother who
Died coming home from deer hunting
　　　　And was not to be spoken of again.
We've buried his body, our tears, his name.

KETTLE MORAINE: WISCONSIN, 1966

In Karl's geology books the grown-up names,
The blissed-out mouthful physical syllables:

Drumlin, esker, lateral moraine,
Kame and kettle, yazoo stream,
Dolomite escarpment, recessional moraine . . .

Inside a power, walking along hogsback ridges,
Their steep sides ancient creek beds deep within
A long-gone glacier I could feel, the dumb muscle

Pressing over the old land, a continent of ice
Dragging itself south an inch a year . . .

And I could see that dull bully
Slowly shouldering through,
Pounding iron-ore mountains
Into rocky fields fit to till,
Digging deep into the soft flesh
Of the continent and leaving great
Gaping holes for the earth
To fill with meltwater.

My oldest brother's book said
Always remember HOMES:
Huron Ontario Michigan Erie Superior

LABOR DAY

Yesterday these same two off-white seagulls
were merely displaced garbage birds too dumb
to find the landfill dumped across the river
but today they're transforming, damned angelic
scribing a sweet hole in the after-summer blue
above St. Joseph's quarried blocks of local basalt—
these birds are surely a sign and for once
I don't care what they're saying, they're just good
avains turning on air as always, today they mean
simple joy, full to the skin as I am this sun-up
with sap, a state not wholly unrelated to last
night's foot rub or the incandescent hour thereafter
when she said yup, that's the first of September,
so I remembered to call my dad and say happy birthday
and somehow he's 64 and out in the garden where he's
happiest on a new cordless phone and getting owly
about late tomatoes and some shyster with wormy corn
wanted five bucks a dozen and he had to pay it,
family picnic coming up and he always does the corn
but I hear him smile as he tells it, what a crock
he says and I can hear that he's sober and it's ten
here so that's noon, Wisconsin, that's doing good.
Mom's better since her bypass, getting her color
and they both ought to quit smoking he supposes . . .
well I love you, Dad. Right now, I wanted to say
I love you and mean it and forget about waiting
in the car at Smoley's and he says yeah, yeah,
you too and maybe he wants to forget my telling him
to kiss my ass, what do you know about it and there's

another call coming in, he has to go and we both
say I hope to see you soon and for what it's worth—
all we have, never enough—we mean that too.

Complacencies of the pee-jays, and late
Instant Folgers and fried liver sausage on the sofa,
And the green and gold of the Packers
On the black-and-white Zenith swirl and sweep to remove
The unholy husk of weekday work and hustle.
He listens to Stan Getz and Pee Wee Hunt
A little, and he ignores the dark
Encroachment, that old catastrophe, for a moment,
As a horn blues up the living room.
The smell of the liver and the sweet, clear notes
Seem things singular, declaring themselves alive,
Skimming lightly across untested water.
The day unwinds like a funeral procession with no corpse,
Breathing for the sake of our own breaths
Through the all-forgiving air, on thick ice,
Alive for the dream of the deep pool below.

EXPENSE OF THE HEART

BEFORE FIRE

Housesitting for friends to save July's rent
I pull two pairs of carrots, brooding flesh
Dense and bartered for like all salvation,
Temporary and coming at someone else's expense,
The four orange frontmen of the apocalypse

Proclaiming the nascent final fire,
One bad uncle of which is the local
Bitterroot Forest aflame, a threat
So real I have to ignore the rather
Too-obvious pall over this borrowed

Valley, this sublime short-term stream
Out the window, these other people's fine
Possessions, the scattered galaxies of high-
End playthings delivered in well-founded hope
In honor of David, their one-pound miracle

Baby who made it, who beat all the odds,
A sudden reminder of the sentence accorded
Myself by a simple diversion of X and Y,
Of the nonexistent daughter I'll never
Watch dance, or son dip the moon from

Freezing Lake Michigan, an expense
Of the heart not budgeted for,
And so, into the approaching smoke
Must go, to offer what I am:
This mouthful of ashes.

January backyard, blissfully alone with a full bottle
        Of single-batch bourbon and old Mount Jumbo,
That sure dumb knob of reserve that holds back
        Nothing: not the elk that stob the bald hump

Suffused with sky, not common mule deer or buck
        Brush or red osier dogwood or ponderosa pine,
Not even the scrappy tom cat Old Joe Frazier
        Skulking down the hill with one milky eye

And a bum hip, ascending the chokecherry tree
        To perfect the one trick left him, the grosbeak drop,
Seed-crackers lured by my feeder reduced to a puff
        Of feathers, a bony mess I pitch to the alley,

And Joe limps off alone to his hillside lair,
        Some stinking hole this whisky wants me in—
I've followed him but can't get in, not yet,
        Discarding my life drop by drop, word by word.

IMPACT

Somebody's daughter on a too-big bicycle
        coming straight at me looks back over her
shoulder and yanks the bike square
        into my Chevy's grill going twenty-five.

She snaps up into the dangerous air
        her mother's been warning about,
hands held out to ward me off,
        face turned sideways into the ripe
melon sound of young bone and flesh.

Her neck jerks as she slides across the glass,
        one bare leg slowly and a filthy tennis shoe
as she becomes a new girl, one who flies
        to me in nightmares to come
and I become the faceless man in her dreams.

Stopped, somebody's hand turns
        the key to "off." Ten feet away
the girl lies perfectly
        still in the ditch as though
I've thrown her there hard
        curled obscenely, one shoe gone.

She staggers to her feet:
        "My bike, you ruined my bike!"
then a scream, another from behind,
        her mother at a dead run half dragging,
half carrying a wild-eyed sister in tears.

A siren, an ambulance backing up,
         paramedics check her ribs for breaks
and smile, everybody shaking their heads,
         embarrassed at the excess concern . . .
the driver touches my arm, she's all
         right, she's going to be all right.

Then why strap her down to a stretcher?
         Why not let the sister ride along?
Her mom wants some insurance information
         but I don't have a thing. She'll take cash.
A soft-eyed cop hands me a clipboard—
         I am Vehicle A. Write it all down?

I hit her.

A block from home near the tarry
         skid marks, kids huddled on bikes
point at my car.

Tim and I walk past a baby in a tall
jar of tea-colored liquid, a precise
oval of skin excised from his chest
to below his navel, intestines coiled
like a string of cartoon sausages.
The professor lectures on female shoulders,
points to a life-sized wall chart like Mom's
old medical book, clear plastic plates
of a man and a woman, side by side,
to peel apart page after page:
the skin, the muscles, the internal organs,
all the way down to the bones.

Through a locked door, a white room
with seven steel tanks on legs.
Tim opens the hinged cover.
"This is Old Joe." They're all
named. A man floats face down
in clear fluid that stings my nose.
His skin's removed, back muscles
ribbed like heavy gray corduroy.
The students point with pencils,
touch him then to turn him over.
Stiff, reluctant, Joe rolls with a quiet
splash. His nose and lips, one eye
his hair: all gone.

There's one picture of my father in Korea—
he kneels, smiling, beer in hand
before long strings of ears the Turks
cut from Chinese corpses.
"That was a long time ago"
is all he'll say.

I wonder who could do this,
strip a man of his skin,
neatly trim his face away.
A medical student, someone like Tim,
or a father in a war?
Or I could, today I could.

ODE TO MY SCROTUM

Old man of the pubis, apple-
Faced and glum as Jehovah, plumb
Bob of my trunk, snout
Of my groin, altar of the first

Scratch of morning, adorable
Cahone holder extraordinaire,
Stone boat, snood-like sackful
Of my worst and best moments

I apologize for twice I have defiled
You with painstaking razor and soap:
Once at a casual request, for lust,
Once for the doctor of vast indifference,

Snick snick, a quartet of bristling
Black stitches and oh how you did
Dilate, wrinkles distended to an eight-ball
Smooth and size, you were made to swell,

Fellow, host of the thistly nubbins that chafe
O! totem O! glorious shifting seedbag,
Unself-conscious sachem of the gonads,
Treasure trove, most tender

And vulnerable storehouse: hurt
Me there and I stay injured,
A bruise like a heart wound, an evening sky:
Deep blue that by morning will yellow.

Pelted with forty-mile-an-hour gravel
The glaciers hauled for punishment
I skid down the dirt road in Wild
Rose Wisconsin on a red plastic saucer
With ten feet of bad rope between me
And the bumper of Jerome Pokorny's
Pontiac, oven mitts for safety gloves,
A paper-bag helmet with racing stripes,
Dipping a shoulder to scuff off the ruts,
The world a telescoped blur of dirt and chrome

And the blistered sled begins to melt
Against my butt, underwear eroded
To cheesecloth, the road a funnel
Fenced by pines, Jerome slows for the final
Turn and I tuck a shoulder, drop my chin
And go for the blind headlong tumble
Toward some indefinite mix of physics
And luck, whatever's at the end
Of a boyhood waiting
For me in the dust.

THE BLACK ROAD

PASTORAL

En route, the silver
car a greasy
      sheen of Kansas insects.
        A couple.
In a stone-pocked
pasture a crow,
      its claws deep
      in a red calf,
           slack and alone,
        tugging off slivers of flesh.
Christ, he
says, why doesn't somebody
      clean that up?
        She nods,
the ragged bird lifts
and returns to pull
      at the tender,
      fly-blown anus.
        A tear carves down
        the ditch of her cheek.

The black road
rises between them.

NIGHT CATS AT THE GRAIN ELEVATOR

Not one black: they don't need it,
these slinks of the evening who wear
their own shadows, eat light

like a cave. Of sound there is
none, each footfall a padded
measure of silence. Their eyes

shine pure and lethal, a feral
purposeful blank stare
that holds no malice, no ruth

just a simple prophecy:
I alone shall survive.
They eat their ill-formed

newborns spine and all with poisonous
teeth and jaws that crush skulls like
candy. Their torn ears are tuned

to the minute clicks of vole claws,
a packrat's clatter and rasp,
the damp pantings of a buried skink.

After years, these cats grow
through their ninth life and become
luminous to each other, levitate

to tread pathways of air, snag
pigeons out of their battering
flight, commute with their dead

and drift without season, saintly,
to where there are no more filicides,
no hunger or abandonment,

where day may not follow,
to the perfect feline dark.

Regal is right: sovereign bird
        enthroned upon a sloping Idaho
Studebaker Hawk, windows blown
        by stray basalt scree, an indecent
hood ornament from above, inbred,
        foppish, stump-dumb as any monarch,
jolting the stubblefield with blue
        that jingles the light, conspicuous
as a pope, weighted by the vestments
        of glamor and willful ignorance, obtuse
and untutored in the hardscrabble rules
        of the goose who pokes the ground nearby
for cast-off grain, the dull, dun gleaner
        who even now swivels his wedge of head
and with a most common hiss and squawk
        hobbles into flight downhill, to the river
and only then does the nonplussed peacock—
        burdened into stupefaction by his own
five-foot anchor of royal beauty—see
        the bobcat, color of dust and weed,
thinking not salvation, not grandeur,
        thinking blood and muscle and bone.

A GOD'S SONG: SHAMIRPET, INDIA

But then some mornings I awake so proud
Of my divinity I feel my horns
Can scoop the disappearing moon and hold it
Where I please. And when the mortals mark

Their foreheads with the ashes of my dung
I know what comfort my existence
lends to lives of dust and hunger.
And when I walk among them all bow low.

No hand is raised to hurry my slow passage.
But when the infidels clamor through the market
My head hangs low, my nostrils in the dust.
They curse my name and lash my flanks with sticks.

They say my flesh could steal from death
A thousand hungry widows. They say
I feed upon the grain of starving children.
They want me gone.
                    But I am not moved.

Fred's pounding the door again, evicted
By his own cat, limestone fists a cartoon blur.
Those mitts were just helpless, up in the air
In Mr. Slate's office as Fred blasted

Out, a transmuted Gleason with a wall
Of frustration that goes back before
The Stone Age started. At home, he hollers
At Barney, who knows like we do that hell,

Fred's not mad at him, he's yelling at the stooge
Inside who can't quite get a handle on the confusing
Quarried blocks of life that come straight to him
And blot out the sun, too big to dodge.

Later, he'll make up with Barney, kiss
Wilma and we'll know he means it. Well
Here's to you, Fred, a toast in your honor,
another insignificant gesture

like beating a door, hoping someone is there,
like falling in love, like saying a prayer.

Jason shoots through soft ice to the hip,
        shoreline slushed-up by sunshine bounced
off basalt, but rock-solid thirty steps out.

There's hooks and sinkers, cotton line, grubs
        gone black in the bucket and shrimp from Jimbo's
Bait. We sing "Go down, green bobber, go down,

baby I'm talkin' 'bout some good-lovin' trout,"
        same old dirge for dead winter as the pileated
rhythm section whops its iron weisenheimer head.

Sweetly the sun bumps the bid up ten degrees
        and the bobbers respond: a couple of muscled
salmonoids jack-knifing on the ice and even

the lean ones are longer in these piney woods
        of the Clearwater Range on the first day the light
runs longer than night. One chunky rainbow

horseshoes the air and belly-flops back down
        the hole, trailing slushy clouds of glory. The tongues
of dusk-fueled flames that descend to halo

our skulls as we kneel are bestowed not by some
        spirited dove from without, but rise up wholly
from within.

SOMEONE WAS THERE

MARILYN

Thank god you died
                when you did,
or you'd have ended up
                owning the Florida Marlins
jiggling and bloated and
                afraid of yourself
stunningly drunk of course
                on Boodle's gin
and browned in the tanning booth
                of self-admiration
strolling out for the seventh
                inning stretch with two
fat wiener dogs on diamond
                studded leashes and reeling
through the infield among
                the blushing veterans
and star-popped rookies all
                of whom it's rumored
you'll ball before the first
                ceremonial pitch
wobbling thick amid the leering
                boos you've long
since learned to ignore
                some young Kennedy
panting from the dugout
                made-for-TV movie
on the docket, special guest star.

Or no.

Maybe you'd have saved yourself
                    gone dignified
sober and out of the public eye
                    Norma at the hospice
twice a week quietly caring
                    for the others
we've quarantined by leaving
                    off the love
maybe you'd have met Alex and
                    maybe he'd have known
that someone was there who could say
                    I love you
someone who cared—not me,
                    but a perfect someone.

ESCHATOLOGY (FOR MY SCARS)

All lovely and troubling, puckered
Reminiscences, claiming dispensation
From the plebian indignity of hair,
Unrepentant epistles of misjudgment

And sinister incident, Quisling skin,
Discorporeal mastic memoirs,
Tsk-tskers, teen-boy tyrants,
Memento moi, portenders

Of apocalypse, hobo epidermis
Purplish and sutured but still
Reluctant offspring of surgical
Steel and gut, warlock's kiss,

Palimpsest of consequence,
Scrapbook ticket stubs
Of misery and the terminal
Forgiveness of flesh.

This is goodby I guess, surf-sounding
Hiss and worse, the loss of the regular
Rhythmic tick and pop of a scratch

On a vinyl round—related by name
To the grape, through the twisting vine—
Lost to the Darwinian march

Of Hi-Fi, 8-track, cassette and now CD,
Digital, gone the sound itself deftly
Pressed into the generous flesh

Of a wax master, this new music so
Perfect with a hard-wired heart
And I for one am sorry to see you

Go, static, those tragic lapses
A reminder of the glorious hitches
In the soulful swing we call

Our lives and must dance alone
While the orchestra offers up
The blessed heart-wrenchéd

Symphony of our flawed and fatal
Selves, a fugue of forgiveness
For the reckless beauty of imperfection.

WEEDS

Blessed fiend, sultan of the sagebrush
        spotted knapweed of thee I sing,
bowed before your spiked tenacity.

Cousin to other floral marauders,
        unholy cadre we honor with sacred
pagan names: dalmation toad flax

dyers woad, purple looserife, leafy
        spurge, hawkweed, cinquefoil,
hoary cress. Knapweed, you're

a hired gun gone amok, imported
        by beekeepers greedy for late
summer blooms, but soon

you outgrew the pasture
        and blasted free, root-fed
toxins offing all around:

pedestrian bunch grass,
        hyperbolic balsam root,
the range-hardened sage,

croaked by your democratic
        methods—all must die—
just doing what you have to,

doing what you can
        and you have done it all:
invaded, took over,

wiped out the locals
        poisoned the ground
wasted the water

moved west, ever west
        and hell, that's why we fight
so hard to purge you in futile

"War on Weeds" campaigns,
        knowing we'll fail, miraculous
centaura maculosa, impure beast

half human, we love
        and hate you best,
the honeyed weed within.

Implacable, impeccably bereft of even the trace
of ambition and dressed in rare buffoon pantaloons
here they come, feet free-wheeling the bean-filled
sack, dozens of dreadlocked white guys from Sheol,
incubi of pure pachydermal insouciance drunk
on testosterone and heisted microbrew, eyes
a bit greazy from Idaho ditch weed and lack
of sleep, numb from the knees up and grinning
the gap-toothed leer of adolescent fascists,
the rampant extension of a cracked democracy,
hootenanny masochists elastic in their convictions
and damned glad to be here, coiling down Main Street
in packs of six, spilling off the sidewalks
and placidly tying up traffic for miles
grateful as always for deadening gridlock—
kick, kick, the nervous flickering inflections
of ankles and a hip-glancing *pok*, then past,
Beelzebub's bad clowns caterwauling out of town
content this time to scare the curtains
off the windows of responsible fathers
behind which, trembling, the thunderstruck
daughters won't get along with their business
thrilled to the toes by the graceful,
hate-filled spectacle of change.

Puccini and blackberry flapjacks for Sunday
    Breakfast, nothing like opera and real
Maple syrup to goose up your rooster
    A bit, and me and Miss Patience got all
There was to get from that sorry Italian,
    Hitting those high notes like Gary Cooper
At a turkey shoot and her on the drainboard
    Wringing an apron with nothing else on,
And over her shoulder where I have to
    Look to keep from going batshit crazy
Stand Pete and Lady, a matched pair
    Of sideways Clydesdales catching
Every last bit of sun except the one
    Ray that lights her sweet breast
From behind. Good Lord, it's a far
    Better world I go to when I stay home.

THE SIMPLE FACT OF THIS DAY

VAN GOGH IN MONTANA: SEPTEMBER REPRISE

I

Thinking of Theo's last letter, hoofing it
again in well-oiled work boots he's aware
that the weather's been Spanish of late
but today is definitely Dutch: drizzle
seeps through the unlikely blonde copse
of moss-hung larches alongside a sentimental
pond expiring its fine autumnal sigh
of mist and two slick beaver, indolent,
bellied into a sun-draped mud bank
with cattails evangelically blown,
their seeds gone to haloed flinders.
A smolder of birch adorns the pasture
where regal mules gather in oafish clumps
ignoring Appaloosa colts in spanking
piebald faces and spats, genteel
in dalmation blankets. Snow tricks
the Swan Mountains into bringing down
the scented sky, a husk of woodsmoke
heady with all the banked tales of summer,
oracles of winter to come. Yearling
whitetail deer stutter and feint
at the roadside. A slow one shoulders
the ditch, head thrown back with nodding
ravens chuckling at her ribs. In a cleft
of ponderosa pine bark, two thumb-sized
bats, feet up in webbed straightjackets
of flesh. He envies their pure dislocation,

their easy, outsider ways. No one expects
of them anything but horror and this,
with their very lives, they provide.

II

An abandoned orchard spills across
barbed wire, twisted apples drag
the limbs down into Queen
Anne's lace. A blue heron wheels one
tight spiral to a pothole pond unseen
past fieldstone rock piles bruising
with lichen beneath wild grape vines,
leaves the color of dried blood, and snow:
slantwise, ornate, indelible. The air
thickens with chill, his corporeal breath
another body to pass through. He hears
a pneumatic chuff from the dark
between stone slopes, a preposterous
bull moose seven feet at the shoulder
bearing that loopy confused look, nose
groping Vince's scent—a mere human.
The moose returns his mouth to the earth,
tears free moss clumps with a scoff,
and pisses a thirty-second stream.
Vince joins him, proffering his meager
water in kinship before moving on
as the sun casts a salmon-pink sheaf
of light on the luminous hills of shale,
and the simple fact of this day is enough,
if only for this once.

III

Something in him loves a furrow,
plumping the air with the earth's
body smell, even now as snow stains
the jet black hummock of loam . . .
something in his ancient brain that tugs
like a Nordic ache for the gone
and the going. Vince bets the driver
of that propane truck toting
his casual boulder-sized bomb
knows the yank of the ground
on a curve, the Blackfoot River
a finger crooked below, knows
the desire to let go the wheel
and end in flame, not fade, not
simply dissolve. But he holds on,
steers true as Vince does. The bats
he admires as brothers
we'd rather deny, like fathers,
like our own shadow selves.

Mephisto Motors, used parts and whole
wrecks, nine miles out of town,
the handmade I-beam gate patrolled
by a three-legged mongrel, a hundred
pound snarl with bad gums
and oily fur. The boss is in
the shed out back, joining iron
with that resolute blue spark,
no mask, slashing through steel
with a torch, skrick-skrick
and the air zooms from zero
to two-thousand degrees, an unlit
cigar stub tucked into one cheek
and by god he's grinning as he
looks out over his lot: beaten-
down Firebird, a misspent Fury,
Gremlin in decorous rust, seats
blown like a milkweed pod, black
Falcon up to its trunk in muck.
"Your car?" He hacks and spits
a thunderous gob. "That fucking car's
bad meat. You're lucky if I take it
off your hands. What do you mean,
what'll I *give* you for it?"
He's a perfect mimic, pisses
your words down into the mud.
"Step inside, we'll talk."
In the shed, he chucks a log
into the oil-drum stove.

His gut shifts suspiciously
under his coveralls, something
inside him alive and unwell.
"Listen. You should buy that
Gremlin. I'll make you a deal.
You want it or not?"
Whatever it is,
it's too much to pay,
but you can't say no:
you want him to like you,
to ask you to stay.

You might come here some day in a blizzard.
Say your wife broke down. The last good fish
you caught was years ago. You drive this road
plowed out by the inept, past parks
with frozen gates, an outhouse that's thawed, the tortured skies
above local fishermen stiff in open pickups.
Only augers are kept sharp. The pails
upturn by the dozens. They're all prisoners
of the still bobbers, not knowing what they've done wrong.

The principle supporting emotion now
is boredom. Bored with the various crusts
the lake sends, bored with the snow,
the Five in Aggregate Limit, the best-liked fish
that were always biting yesterday. One good
nibble can't wipe the boredom out.
That day last February, eight silver salmon,
ice thick up to the springs—
all memory dissolves in a snowblind haze,
in apocalyptic white you know will slick the roads
into two ruts back to town,
two downward ditches, your huge Buick in collapse
for a hundred thousand miles that won't break finally down.

Isn't this your life? That last fish
still drying on the smoker? Isn't this ice fishing
so pointless, the mealworm simply seems
a pure distraction: jig and nothing comes?
Doesn't empty water sing? Are cabbage weeds

and corn sufficient to uphold a lake,
not just Georgetown, but lakes
of hogbellied trout, good weather and fish
the world will never let you catch
until the lake you live on dries up?

Say no to boredom. The old man, twenty
when he started, still fishes
although he sometimes naps. Someday soon,
he dreams, I'll catch a ten-pounder and wake up.
You watch his bobber. You're jigging for yourself.
The car that brought you here still runs.
The money you buy bait with,
no matter how it's earned, is gold
and the rainbow that slaps the lake
is splendid and its red stripe lights the ice.

"FISHERMAN FOUND ADRIFT ON ICE FLOE, LAKE SUPERIOR"

His shiner minnow, lightly hooked, will swim
Below him as he drifts, a continent
Cut loose from moorings. For now, why not fish?
Night's locomotive pulls into the station of darkness.

This hole connects him to the lake, a circle
All the way down to hard bottom. His ice
Raft's edges are softened by warm air. Murky,
It slicks his cheek with a veil of moist lace.

At home, the circle waits inside the track.
His train rolls slowly past familiar buildings,
Nice and easy around the bends, comes back
Soft, like sleep, as though bidden, and willing.

If Vera thinks of him at all, she'll know
That he is anchored, steady, to this hole.

POINT OF DISAPPEARANCE

The plane refuses

to let the sun
go down—it's

a red half-penny

cut off by
the puny world.

Up is all this

pilot knows:
poor Georgia

reduced to a skein

of tinny wet snakes
that thread together

the on-switching

towns. Someone
lives in each, awake

and aware of just who
they are. The scattered
houses flicker below,

blue-gold and

seductive
like freakish deep-
sea creatures fluorescing.

In the time
it takes to rub
my eyes we're

over Memphis

and the purling

oxbow lakes of

        the Mississippi,

     which at the horizon

  looks even more

         drifty than the

muslin

mist we're slipping

through. At the edge

      of earth and sky

    a carmine stew

  of clouds confuses

        the issue, the

point

of which just now eludes

me: where the world

     ends, and I begin.

SAVING GRACE

When the choir leaned into Amazing Grace
the bass section billowed through first
and hummed inside me, a deep-chested rumble
of crew-cut uncles and the gas station owner
from town, dark robes hitched and dipped
from thrown-back shoulders. Soprano aunties
under beehive hair piles cut in the sweet
and lonesome sound that shivered our backbones.

I didn't quite get what "genuflect" meant
or exactly why my grandma rolled hard
beads most nights in her rocker
but I knew what I felt at Good Shepherd
was holy and was inside the priest
and even the old German farmers,
stiff faces softened in song.
I had to learn those words like the choir,
to sing without a glace at the book
so even God could see the holy in me.

When we shuffled back from Communion,
the kneeling part, Grandma pressed
her forehead against the golden wood
of the pew before us, moving her lips
in tiny winces. Slipping the book
with the right words into my pants
I prayed please God don't let me
get caught, I'm doing this for you.
Under the late-night quilt with a stolen

flashlight I squinted every word in,
then repeated each verse in the dark.

Next Sunday standing tall on the kneelers
I belted Amazing Grace straight out,
every syllable strung in order. But
stopping to think, I lost the shiver
of music in my body, my rosary
of words gone bitter and common.

Then the choir sang through me again
and I felt the pulse, still there
inside the language. I sat back,
rocked on the hard pew wrapped
in the blanket of rhythm and vowels,
divine in the dialect of sound.

ACKNOWLEDGMENTS AND NOTES

My thanks to the editors of the publications in which these poems first appeared, often in highly altered states:

"Diaspora" and "Weeds" in *Alaska Quarterly Review*

"Kettle Moraine: Wisconsin, 1966" in *The Bloomsbury Review*

"Zero Degrees at Georgetown Lake" and "Cold Morning: Weitas Creek, Idaho" in *Cabin Fever*

"Charismatic Hacky-Sackers" and "Pastoral" in *cold-drill*

"Boneyard" in *CutBank*

"Elegy for Album Noise" and "Saving Grace" in *Front Range Review*

"Marilyn" in *Fugue*

"A God's Song: Shamirpet, India" and "Learning from the Dead" in *The Guadalupe Review*

"No Church" in *Northern Lights*

"Night Cats at the Grain Elevator," "Point of Disappearance" and "Reuben, Sunday Morning, 1967" in *Poetry*

"Aubade for a Garment Bag" and "Van Gogh in Montana" in *Rendezvous*

"Bad Neighborhood" in *Seattle Review*

"Peacock Rex" in *Talking River Review*

"Impact" in *Tar River Poetry*

"Ode to My Scrotum" in *The Temple*

"In Praise of Abandon" in *Willow Springs*

"Fisherman Found Adrift on Ice Floe, Lake Superior" and
"Turning to Roses: Montana War Memorial,
Missoula, 1990" also appeared in *In Other Words:
An American Poetry Anthology*

"Night Cats at the Grain Elevator," "Ode to My Scrotum"
and "Reuben, Sunday Morning, 1967" also
appeared in the *Pacific Northwestern Spiritual
Poetry Anthology*

"Ode to My Scrotum" was printed letterpress as a
broadside by Fameorshame Press

"Reuben, Sunday Morning, 1967" is an homage to Wallace
Stevens's "Sunday Morning"

"Zero Degrees at Georgetown Lake" is an homage to Richard
Hugo's "Degrees of Grey in Philipsburg" and "Bad
Neighborhood" is in memoriam, Richard Hugo

"Van Gogh in Montana" is for Marnie Bullock Dresser

"Last Names" is for David Long

"Night Cats at the Grain Elevator" is for Robert Wrigley

Thanks to my parents, Mary Ulah (Flanders) Held and Reuben
John Held; and to my brothers and sisters: Karl, John, Jim,
Dave, Kathy, Joe, and Suzanne.

Thanks to my teachers, especially Phil Zweifel.